Eardrum

By the same author:

Poetry

Faultlines (with Y. Christianse and N. Krouk)

The Great Wall of Instinct

In the Cage of Love's Gradings

Be Straight with Me (for teenagers)

Sensual Horizon

The Human Project: New and Selected Poems

Ground

Anthologies

Midday Horizon (ed. with P. Boyle and M. Bradstock)

Harbour City Poems: Sydney in Verse 1788–2008 (ed.)

Contemporary Australian Poetry

(ed. with J. Beveridge, J. Johnson and D. Musgrave)

Criticism

Microtexts

Aphorism

Neat Snakes

Other

Ngara: Poems, Essays and Meditations (ed. with John Muk Muk Burke)

Schubert Sonata D. 960

With quiet assurance,
the firm, hairless tentacles
press
and start off on their walk:
step out with unshowy flourish –
calm, unsolicitous trills . . .

off on their long, mountain passage –
plateau-paths coded in ink-marks at night –
a silent and neuron-poised hand . . .

replotted now upon keys
and in aural synapses –

and in those dumplings where intervals
translate as onwardness, tenderness, waste.

Brahms

In Brahms' world, kindness was possible.
There were flowers in the wood,
the conservatory. The composer
looked out over laneways where sun
starked and haloed the branches
all day.
        At any one moment,
the woman on whose shapely hands
the light fell was just leaving –
but that did not lessen his offer.
In these rooms, the language was music,
and music forgives.

        Though it cannot un-know:

the kinder the music,
the sharper the chill of foreboding.

Brahms understood that he came
at the end of the tale: harmonies stretched
in pursuit of more power all led neatly
to fractures and vacuums. They were ripe
with the terror and grief his successors
would braid.

        Still, he insisted you walk
in his rose-scented garden.

It was beautiful there, in that light.

And how could he contemplate leaving?

Who knew what came next?

Ländler

They have gathered
on a little starlit ridge, above the war:
to dance, while the fiddlers play ländler –
affairs of the heart, re-arranged by hard work;
youthful importance re-sized by the depths of the sky.
Sometimes the ländler are sober,
and sometimes they pick the pace up.
What does it matter to these feet?
All human burning sounds wistful, from so far away.

Nor does it matter
if language will not save the dancers –
meaning seep out of their daydreams like moisture from clay –
the music is cheerful to dance to,
their partners polite.

In time-frames elsewhere,
there are pageants and stern demonstrations.
Bold spirits make bolder speeches, write luminous proofs.
For all of their vehemence,
each will revert, in the end, to the bench on the corso –
sit by themselves, in the sun, feeding crumbs to the birds.

The dancers step neatly round bomb-sites.

Their daily achievements will not flare as headlines;
their courteous ways shed no blood.

But their dancing is strange as a clock-face –
as water – or story – this modest, numeric delight.

Shostakovich Trio, Opus 67

When the bones are all dust,
and the crimes of the tyrants forgotten –
the new-land graffiti
by which they'd hoped history might thank them
one paragraph long, in a musty, old book –
what else is left
but the dances and airs
of the few who could weigh what they saw –

and still remain standing,

and still tap and shuffle their grief?

The Young Lady Ventures *Der Kukkuk*, By Abt

— Wahroonga, c1920

Curtains and tapestries;
porcelain; cosies and lace.

And, by the keyboard –
Kukkuk   Kukkuk –
an arc of display
so refined
that it does not exist.

The path to the asymptote
stops at the shuddering bosom:

> where the sighs of desire
> meet the sound-waves of art
> and implode.

Elsewhere in the city,
a purpose need not be mistaken –

> *a need*
> *can look a longing*
> *in the eye.*

But here,
in this cell of proprieties,
the dapper young men,
with their earnest, well-funded proposals,
must knight-skip and blink
round a moat of disjunctions –
and even then
not-think the prize:

cunningly elsewhere, away,
in the virtual dimension of art –
though touching each guest so beguilingly –

Kukkuk   Kukkuk

Bach

Just as the war
between knowing
and dancing
would lurch,
like a fate,
towards knowledge:

Bach
made it sound
as if nothing
need keep them apart.

The Form

Josef invented a form.

Which he found
could be streaked with a shadow —
and *that*
made it
okay for big people too.

And then,
Wolfgang saw,
you could make this form walk
down a rope
between darkness and light.

Which,
Ludwig grasped,
could be led to a cliff, *fff,*
where a claim might be made . . .

And so for each adept:
each new suite of tricks for the loom —

till the weave could not take anymore —

till chaos poured in through the fissures:
splinters and subwoofage,
harrowings, gobbets of squid . . .

Dark the whole world:
until someone arrived
with a shape full of new possibilities —
in which —
good minds saw, straightaway —

a minimal shading
might offer some depth, credibility . . .

The Concert

No wonder there's so much kerfuffle:

　　　　evening dress,

　　　　maestro's spak hair;

　　　　divisions of frowns at the ready –
　　　　against the surprise-raids of Cough …

Row after row of good judges –
who've travelled so far
in pursuit of firm answers …

whose questions are starting to fray.

　　　　Good hall, acoustics –
　　　　a tomb newly varnished …

Air-Pollock tune-ups.

Two taps　　　　and then Simon says *Go!*

　　　　For this is the concert –
　　　　(again!)
on which everything teeters –

　　　　tonight,
a unique range of talent
　　　　　　will try to establish
　　　　for once and for all:

　　　　that they –

and all those who are present –

        are not simply earnest –

are more than the void.

Mistah Lurv-Man

Straight up, he winks at the crowd:
misery first,
just the hint of an uncontrolled breath –
just the quietest start
to a stage-managed rout –
mute horns, half-clutches of grief. . .
But then: and before the third song,
it is time to stand up.
How did he get there so quickly?
Suddenly, nothing can hold him.
He's off – he is yanking the cord.
And his crotch – it's too tight!
He must take off his jacket.
He's got to declare himself –
ME! BABY! ME! LOOK-A-ME!
The crowd – it agrees: and with feeling.
They're boppin' wide, shaking free.
They're down there: working those bodies!
And up there! Mouthing those dreams!
He's singing *close*, singing *only*;
he's singing *always* and *win*.
He knows that *this* dance-hall
knows what it wants, *and* with rights.
It's hearing *special*, and *need you*;
it's hearing *mine* and *belong* –
higher – like *mine*↑ – and with encores.
    Till . . . in the limp scrum post-climax:
when everyone's masks have blown loose –
and all needs are on show –
what can we do
except eddy away
into all the impossible options
of love cast as proof?

The C20th

The Walk to the Paradise Gardens

Knoxville: Summer of 1915

Takemitsu's *Rain Tree*

Sculthorpe's *Island Dreaming:*

intent on our crimes,
nobody noticed
we had also realised
a non-triumphal,
non-narrative happiness
for the first time since the polyphonists –

and as an ecstasy of the earth's.

Randy Newman

You want to scream so loud
the bastards can't stop up their ears.

Make things so clear
they can't bear to recall what they've done.

But you have some idea of your limits.

So you opt to try worming
inside their thick heads
with innocuous Tin Pan distractions –

   trapped

between rage
at monstrosity –

   and dismay

at the use of your gifts.

1956: Graduation Ball

The Board,
and all their wives,
and all the notables,
have breathed in
and squeezed into waistlines –
breathed out and plumped up their suits . . .

steadied to stern
beneath hairspray and Brylcreem and pin –

sworn – without swear-words – at stoplights,

poufed into place, and peered out,
from their stage on the stage –

No! their horn-rimmed glasses say,
and
No! their jowls agree:

Our sexuality never existed.

Bass counts it in, *One-and-Three. . .*

Clapping

I clap —

join the onrush of hands:
        wind beating paper and sticks
        through the sine-waves of roar.

Beaming, the tenor bows low.

But where did the marvellous go to?

When did it duck
and re-surface as debt and exchange?

Hornsby Fountain

In Hornsby Shire,
Art's when the man from the council
addresses the chore of the bells.
He puts on his raincoat and hat,
& steps up to their udders –
props up his plastic
and enters the zone – though not wildly,
as Liszt might have done –
but boldly, with firm, mature tuggings –
schemas of favourite fun-tunes,
one squint at a time. . .
The water transcends up the buckets –
off into see-saws & back out of mouths
in a flourish of wide-gape emissions.
All the proud ratepayers watch him –
while all the proud bushland inhabitants
focus elsewhere[1] – though eagle stares back,
and refuses to blink at their rapture –
at mid-morning aesthetes
transported by frissons not unlike
those prompted by first hits of Mexican Gold.

1. The fountain is home to a comprehensive range of animal statuary.

From: The Australian Musical Almanac

The Canterbury-Bankstown *Agnus Dei*,
      for twelve-part voice –
leaving no stone unturned, for the team.

Front-lawn acoustic duets –
      Cunning Tips for New Members –
            in a false Irish brogue
            by the Speaker and Whip:
with a beer – and a plate of fresh pikelets.

The RBA Activ-Bod Beats Kit.

Medleys from ladies
      whose past wars on Twitter
      are no bar to gigs
in the Power Workshop:
            Zen your Love Blue.

            The role of Violetta,
as interpreted by Smurf and Robbo's crew.

Belt-me-a-Love-Song brain-implants
      for bashful koalas.

The Fisher's-Ghost-Discovers-Johnny-Farnham
      Moonlight Tours.

      Pilots
   for the project
to revitalise the city's drains with fado.

The murder-ballad rewrite of the anthem.

The School-Song Eisteddfod for unsteady, hormonal groans.

The Singer

She has kicked off her high heels
and let down her hair –
pillows and shirts down her front...
a length of old flex for a mike, and –
the rest of the evening
leans out into blues –
waddles and squawks
like a comedy drunk,
tough-talks like Tart-in-a-Pub:
late night graffiti –
unsinging – undancing –
the roles she believes in all week.

Even when everyone heads off to bed,
she will stay up, and shuffle, and tilt:
throw back her shoulders
and keen – her eyes shut –
hard, against those she is trapped by;
low, against those she loves best.

Symphony

Like a small girl singing to herself,
the violins begin as if unmindful –
but how quickly stumble
on pulses, accretions, of need.
Winds enter: air playing games
between leaves – unfocused mischief
on sun-vintaged steps to the lake …
until, intertwining with strings –
as if they had tripped to a tendency –
no: a necessity – there all the time –
they suddenly knit and push forward
to pull for their climb…
By the time the whole brass
has so publicly aired its intentions,
there is no other choice
but to strive for those permanent heights.
If this is impossible, that is the knowledge
the instruments carve into sorrow.
Nor does it matter the audience knows
it's a trope. They're too intent
on the resonance bowed from these hollows.
The lower strings bellow with increase.
They modulate – aching, impatient:
up towards triumph, where death lives;
up towards winning: immaculate, plausible, vague.
Up to the throne room; release from the flux;
the height of the rock-face
confirmed by crescendos: drums joining in
as the giant chords lock
into all the illusions of key shifts;
up to the cliff-edge, the moment –
a pause for some piccolo griefs –
and then the great launch

of the final, tiered claim: that we're home,
that we're on higher ground.
That we don't have to live
in the difficult rippling of now.

Mahler In Midsummer

The Mahler is vanishing:
out through the glare and the tinder –
bottlebrush, leaf-crumble,
jigsaws of litter and shade.

The sighs, the cascades of regret,
are dispersing through anhydrous forms.

To have wanted so much.

To have thought your desires so important.

The great dream of being beyond terms
is making its exit:

the sky is absorbing the trope
of arriving in heaven by tiered modulation;

the planet forgets, in the utterance,
every vast plea.

This is the new land –
where no god or talent
will ground the child's special petition.

Perhaps we could dance spaces jointly
if selves are provisional.

Perhaps there is room for us all
if the self has lost faith in the empire of love.

The Goldberg Variations

Everything negotiates with silence. Is silence itself.
I always forget this so quickly.
Not like Bach's keyboard works.
They sound like someone attending as thinking unfolds:
listening as phrases – Bach's thoughts – make their way
out of absolute dark and as simply return;
the rest of the household in bed now – a few
distant footsteps, the fires merest ashes and ghosts.
A just apprehension which briefly releases the listener
from self's tireless screws: a cadenced memorialization
of perfect resumptions.
It's not just the Bach. There are others: Bartok string-duos;
the duets of Louis and Ella – simple works, some of them,
free of the pleadings of fetish, the elbows of need.
What liberation they offer is just a construction –
a reading that says things can both ache with grace
and be nothing at all. Still – we are so steeped in ego:
so much that drives us slews out into angers –
the paced, inadmissible boiling of sensible minds.
All gestures have a trajectory. It's just that,
to make something – anything – happen,
requires such inelegant fierceness, such child-like display.
How could I ever proceed with Bach's evenness?
How could I write and be wise?

Caravan Park

Its arrival, as always, unnoticed, longing builds
out of the ether – Saturday, mid-afternoon.
Blackbutts and paperbarks climb through the light
that defines them. Or lean to the perfect reflections
of trunks in dark pools.
                              Eaten by tristesse –
inconsummate story – the people seem less real
than these trees: vanquished by metaphor –
wraiths, dreaming rank, dreaming luck. Someone
plays loud, tinny rhinestone. Yearning
and grief rise to climaxes, yearning and grief.
But make no impression on mirror-recessions
of swamp oak. Nowhere to go but the next song.
Nowhere to finish but new absence, over again.
Lack's broken record fades seamlessly
out through the trees which are neither themselves
nor like anything else.

Hawkesbury River

Head full
of the 'permanent music'
of *Cosí*,
I sit on the steps
of the old, disused wharf,
gaze across shallows
at Long Island –
pipes by the tracks,
tilted hulls;
whistling kites
quartering gleams –
while intimate winds
chill my face
and start working away
at my shoulders,
my skull,
and its classic refrains.

The Bach Chorale

They are practising a Bach chorale at Hermannsburg.

Unresolved triads float out past the she-oaks:
a music of journeys,
where each of the chords leads elsewhere.

It has sailed round the world as a magical hachure.

And now, it is out of the box.

Where will it go to tomorrow?

It pleases them, trying to please the good pastor.

They lean into cool, desert air, and they whole-body-listen –
singing themselves, so attentively, out of their lives.

The Country Where Nobody Sings

The songbirds began here.

The first people sang.

The new people too –
they were still singing down to the war.

Then, bit by bit, we shut up.

Because all our songs were sung for us;
because songs were spotlights – and not invitations;
because we could not afford suffering;
because singers lived in a high-life of low-life elsewhere –

because we'd grown careful round meanings –

tongue-music dried into syntax.

For the kids, for results, for immunities:
we sifted conclusions – and tightened our throats.

Prose settled over our lives like a cloud of unbeing.

We would make ourselves still for the fine print,
and stare out at love. . .

Once there'd been tyrants in mills who'd admonished all singing.

We do not need them: we govern ourselves.

Now we always think before we speak.

Now that we care for our stories like courtroom exhibits.

Now we can find every reason – but reason to sing.

Hesitating Blues: W.C.Handy

Trummy Young growling
       while Barney unleashes
the birds of desire round the moon –

then Louis cuts in, with the details:

How long has the phone line been down now?
      How long will she still hesitate?

At which they take off into frolics of yearning:
      blithe misereres
           and bright flares of absence –

     high, wailing gambols of grief.

Ariana

Tribute Concert, Manchester, 2017

Who just keeps on singing
and wearing those pants –
making those sweet, funky moves –

as if the fans' *likes*
were the project that mattered –

as if those hot dance-steps
had nothing to do
with the terrorist's choice of location –
for reasons that neither the bomber,
nor she, could admit.

Disjunct

From Wagner
to Debussy,
             Satie
      to Takemitsu,
the ratio of sound to silence shrinks:

till nothing en-islands all notes —
         and the valencies fray.

Star-flakes can make gorgeous sounds.

But they don't drive the song
as the body once did, with its needs.

Where flesh
had been ground for connectedness,
the world and our lacks are no longer conjunct:

    who set needs aside
    in the search for the facts;

    who would not let interests
    take measurements;

    who'd hammer for silence in court,
    that the claims might be heard —

    who still have to manage the mineral animal,
    stumbling along, with its grin. . .

You can plink the crystal dark of disembodiment.

And there goes the Clumsy One,
lurching through beds. . .

Now: play me a song that sings both.

Two Dylan Poems

I: Dylan

That street-smart, cantorial voice, Bob —
measuring out, like your brothers —
Reznikoff, Ginsberg – Levine –
its cracked, harlequin griefs . . .

For the rest –
there was humour –
once humour had something to bite on;
and grace:
where the pain might relent –
the self be translated from victim to guest –
the sinner permitted
to walk in the shadowless room.

That, after all, was the point.

That things mattered: the lost loves, evasions;
confessions, betrayals, retreats.

When the radio said
we were free to invent the whole world now:
you said such stories were stage-business – alibis, smoke –
in the land of last things.

That Lincoln County Road *was* Armageddon. . .

I think of all the fans who simply got you:

the boldness
that never could save us;

the moments of virtue –

the droughts in between.

Of how,
despite a lifetime of credentialling,
we turn and touch our lack, for something real:
the place the heart leaves, in the first place,
the place it ends up.

II: The Old Songs (A Note With Some Burnt Cd's)

For Julia and Ian

The first time I heard *Rolling Stone*,
we were driving home, sunburnt and tired,
in a placid ex-colony
no God of Endings had heard of.
No. Someone was driving us. We would have still been fourteen.
I didn't know *missalonely*. Who *mystery tramp* might have been.
But understood – just – they were versions of who we might be.
And then someone played *Gates of Eden* –
all gestures folding to wastes that I hadn't imagined. . .
howls that made sense of a world beyond aprons and bowls;
Johanna's streets of lost love –
where meaning left trails of dead matches when romance leant in.

I've still got no clue how an art-work defines what it needs to,
but these pieces did: a shape
to the guesswork of boys on the outskirts of town –
on the edge of the world.

And now you replay them.

That same power. That same invitation –
to share in the starkly imagined – its merciless grace:

an offer your grief may refuse now –

the way that it holds us aside and too dark-slow to enter –
unable to breathe for the presence of those who can't talk.

I hope not.

I hope they still come with their hard-boiled communion.

While grief works its channel.

Until you can meet it on terms.

Rock/Rock'n'roll

It didn't take long
for the whitefolks
to recast
the backbeat and bounce
of the new rock'n'roll
to the statements-with-mojo of rock —

to winkle it loose
from the body —
and off into word.

Hey, says the body,
a-wriggling
and shaking:
These lyrics are only for fun.

But how hard was that
for the slow-burning ones to accept?

Jack

i.m. John 'Jack' Adams 1905-1988

He would dress in the darkness,
and make his way down
through the echoes and gleams of the Yard:
climb into floorlessness –
crouch there, aloft and adrift,
while he soldered ships' brains.

Those were the days of class warfare –
of Dads who would not put
one ha'penny down
lest their sons became better than they.

Nothing for tutoring:
You didn't tell me he charged!

Nor for his music:
his Communist father would keep
the piano Jack bought – and that only he played.

So he took on more pupils
while plaster Olympians
frowned at the earnest, wrong man.

And he kept up his speed –
while the metronome laughed.

And he wore gloves at work
so his eloquent fingers
would not be ashamed in clean rooms.

But then war, with its moraines for choices.

And the years, after that, of hard peace.

So he never became a conductor.

How could a dockyardie
ever become a conductor?

All he could do
was to make what he could of it:
leaven – with working-class zen –
his difficult journey to dance-steps –
a progress for grief and good cheer –
like Beethoven's brave allegretto[1].

1.i.e. of the Seventh Symphony – one of his favourite pieces.

The Symphonists

The symphony was a test:
a god-plain Childe Rolandes must cross –
knights of the score and the baton;
knights of the woodwinds and knights of the brass –
while pages in cloakrooms peeked out
at the un-knightly crush;

a metaphor-cavalry – up, and away –
on the god-steps the next phrase must utter;

an auditory mirror, for adults –
by which one might measure the god one contained:
a spirit-assessment by vigour and tact in the fiddles,
by grunt in the bass.

Till – sooner or later –
as Rolande had done, long ago –
the claimants arrived
at the cliff-face of Ultimate Things:
a trumpet, perhaps – more sforzando –
then: storm-winds of urgent repeats –
banging away – for a sign – for a path up the rock. . .

Now, it's the music without claims that haunts me –
which does not implode seeking *home*.

Wrong dreams laid bare,
the great scores were statements grown frantic –

pools, where the heart's lies grew clear. . .

Mighty approaches. But failures as vast as invention.

As wrong as a gesture can be.

And as kind. And as true.

Arcs

That great downward arc in our mood –
from masses for Sun-Kings,
or *God-likes-strong-tribes-Hallelujahs*
in praise of Culloden –
to harmonies frayed like belief:
allegro barbaros that rage as skies darken. . .

But counter-arcs too:

like faint shafts of sun in the forest –
respites from ego,
eyes that would startle and flee –

that dared not remain –
there was nowhere, back then, that they could;

(that did not contribute
to anyone's notion of self)

but that swarmed, all the same –

until, bit by bit,
there were tunes free from status –
Poulenc, with crackers at carnies;
Britten, on Midsummer's Eve –

a music released
from its comic-book triumphs:

a bedrock without a home-key.

Not much to build on, but all we had left
once the claims of the tribe had been shredded –
its legends rewritten as crime-scenes –
the idea of victory scattered like flakes of dried blood –

all we could trust –

who may never, again, build
on anything more than the void,
and the light it devours.

The Uses Of Music

To scare the shit etc.:
Pirate drums. Taiko.
The bloodscent-excitements of beating the Great Khan's battue.

The side-drums of redcoats. The pipes of the clansmen.

Long nights of war-chants, narcotics and rattles with claws.

Peruperu: hakas for battle.

Howls which reprise how one tore out the heart of the fiend.

Toots to impress on the vanquished
the scale and finesse of your military's tactics.

Choruses which solemnize
the highway from the ruler to the god.

Trumpets, to usher embroidered stoles into the palace.

Frissons of bells
and The Gong
for His Most Serene Smile.

Loud, urgent, *authentic* favourites,
to wind up the faithful, for Big Data's key-words.

High voices, pendulous strings –
to float in the candidate's family-soft views about tax.

  The prelude of the softness of the nappies.

  The nocturne of the smoothness of the oil.

Shouts of belonging and triumph –
to imprint the crew-cuts away from Bohemian whispers.

National nasal drones.

Drum-rolls and swells –
to fill voids of enlargement.

Tuttis of proof and undoing –
appogiaturas converging in waterfall fifths.

Screams of endearment – to set the young screaming.

Bass: to encourage the hips.

The mœbius-larynx of loss and desire –
so we see –
          from both sides of the mirror –
                    how this is one sorrow.

Bare chords, on afternoon plains:
heart-maths, to offer the cloud-shadows
versions of home.

The casuarina undersighs of memory.

Tatters of song in the desert of pitiless light,
where humans once – having invented a music for joy –
had prayed to the thin, steep ascent
for the privilege of a hearing.

II

Minims

Punk: when 'wanna screw,
wanna screw, right fucking now,'
was *a moment of cultural significance*.

~

Perhaps jazz
blows happiness
so well
because the body
makes no claims
and has no memory:

whereas rock –
which begins in the word –
must measure itself
against statements
of hope and desire.

~

While Furtwängler conducted *Götterdämmerung*,
the Air Force Transport Band played *In the Mood* –
as the monomaniacal vision gave way
before camps full of soldiers
with only one thing on their minds.

~

Few listen to instruments –
other, that is, than as décor –
for story or shopping or song.

~

Sinatra:

This is as much
as a man should be willing to do:
a good suit –
attention – and style –

the tab for the meal –

then the shtick about love –

                    and that's it:

now it's up to the broad.

~

Growls, howls and grunts for the metal-boys.
Tantrum-importance for punks.
A box of self-pitying noses and lips for the crooners.
Face-paint for emos' hurt hearts. . .

None of which leads
to the difficult commons between us.

~

Johnny Cash at Folsom:

Nothing to say
that he *hadn't* done time:
who sourced his validation
in the artefact of authenticity.

~

We prefer the songs of loss
to be sung
by the glamorous and available.

~

In classical music
the lips move,
the fingers, the lungs. . .

But the hips must be still,
so the chord has a faux-secure base.

~

Does the trumpeter
really believe
we were born to such brilliance?

~

If desire
is the candour in rock,
it's its limit as well:
where can the third person dwell?

~

English music rarely asks
if the listener is willing to die.

~

Defeated by story's loud claims,
music lost faith in the tale
and began writing poems.

~

Even lovers
cannot occupy
the one identity:

Tristan and Isolde
should have read Heisenberg first.

~

The Aleatory:

In a land
where every note
is without precedent,
what can I build
with my memory?

~

Most invite us as equals.

But some –
like Jim Morrison –
Herbert von K. –
want us to do as they say.

~

It can utter ridiculous things;
be placed
in ironic situations.

But the open voice, itself,
cannot be ironic:

as if, like the mind of a child,
it cannot be divided.

~

Janis:

whose suffering was big enough
for the new, amplified instruments.

~

No post-modernist
flensed *triumph*
as starkly as Ludwig.

~

Oedipus (Stravinsky):

After a century
of composers in search of a home,
Stravinsky struck camp on a bare Greek stage,
where he knew there were none.

~

Chamber Music:

(I)

No longer sure
we were speaking to God,
where else to turn, but to others?

~

(II)

More voices
in a lounge-room
than in a crowd.

~

(III)

Closeness and rub
don't leave spaces for airs –

whoever died
for the claims
of a well-played quartet?

~

In the big-sky lands,
amplifications
and swells are absurd.

~

Westfields
is playing
the Mantovani *Rising Sun* –
the one with the pan flutes:

as with the centre itself,
one must set down the real
at the entrance
before one steps in.

~

There never was a link
between the adagio and the finale.

You cannot explain pain.

~

Northerners do not value emotion less.

They wait –
with that light, and that sky –
until things are propitious.

Is it any wonder
they do climaxes, arrivals – and despair?

~

Jazz rarely asks one to agree.

~

Roots music vanished
about the same time
that the working life
stopped being treated
with any respect.

~

A lyric on the page
is a jelly on the shore.

~

Wagner:

Even when music is recast as language,
it cannot say absolute things.

~

Ligeti, Messiaen:

There are losses in moving so far
from the body's anxieties –
but how could one access such wonderment
hampered by selves?

~

Preludes were one way
of solving the crisis of endings.

~

Brahms, Dvorak:

This is where the modern starts:
after Valhalla fell,
no-one would risk death again
for a chord's resolution.

~

Classic Rock Radio:

Complex inflections –
brave, poignant or *raw* –
having yielded
to slow disappointments –

Classic Rock's playlists
no longer lead anywhere –
but the one place
we'd hoped not to go.

~

Like the drag queen's false breasts,
emotion in art only works if the punter believes.

Then someone invented the musical:

giant breasts everywhere –
staircase and foyer – and circle – and catwalk – and sky!

~

Chopin (I):

Nothing to drive this –
apart from the phrase and its needs.

Are we sure
we can manage it –
beauty's exquisite despair?

~

Chopin (II):

Both intimate and ceremonial:
as if on the threshold
between mind-in-common and self –

but lonely –
its sense of self's fate.

~

Why should the home key prevail?

Where, on this earth,
are things
as we would like them?

~

Contemporary:

Space round every instrument –
we are all individuals now.

~

When the rock-star
turns plump,
and starts smiling,
all the young see
is a guide
who has broken his staff
and torn up his permissions.

~

Violins, says Michael Palmer,
are not to be trusted.

And the lead guitar is?

~

All music's
meant to be heard –
but not much
is meant
to be listened to.

~

From the Beatles' *Bathroom Window*
      to Cocker's;
from Dylan's *Watchtower*
         to Hendrix's –
and then, beyond that,
to stadium drums and vast chords –
            as if, all along, the aim
      had been *heavy* –
not seeing how muscle –
      unleavened –
               bloats
to a cheerless, loud prose.

~

Like the adjectives 'grand' and 'sublime' –
what can one *do* with symphonic capacity?

~

Willie Nelson:

Even
if one sings
outside the song,
the sentiment
can still remain inadequate.

~

The fugue disarms
the statement –
and its chasms –
with an invite to a dance.

~

Così:

In which the credulity of ears
plays host
to the credulity of hearts.
~

Opera:

Why should the young
pay attention
to this sensuality –
lost in their own?

~

Bowie (I):

The needs of the glamorous
may be less visceral
but their pain is still real:

the performative
must still give way
before the limits of performance.

~

Bowie (II):

Who first encountered stardom –
and its ally, deep space –
as the beautiful boy, in the clubs.

~

Forbes cited the Ramones –
for their energy –
their freedom from afflatus.
But died before Johnny –
pure, driven, amoral –
returned to the planet as Trump.

~

The drums
to which we march
are not so different
from the dance-beats
that arouse us.

~

Nat King Cole
(*d. throat cancer, aged 48*)

Who resisted, all his life,
with smoke in hand –
        along the tightrope
of that warm and measured voice.

~

No resolutions
in scores for the urban life:
only exhaustions.

~

Variations:

An early post-modern form –
no single version takes precedence.

~

The applause,
one assumes,
is for the beauty of the singing –
not the pain it lays bare.

~

Slow is the tempo of interiority –
body has slowed down enough
to be conscious – *self*-conscious:

now we can measure the weight of things –

now we can grieve.

~

When the tall claims of narrative failed,
Diaghilev came, with the gift of the dance –
as others had done, years before –
allemandes, chaconnes:

that *having-to-think-of-the-other's-next-moves,*
that *footwork-which-renders-them-visible* –

reciprocal offers
by which selves are lost and retrieved;

exchanges in which we are grounded:

who must learn, and re-learn,
that the solo trajectory flares into ash on its grid.

~

So what
that popular music
speaks only
to attractors and attracted?

Since when
has *merely human*
been of interest to the young?

~

Without claims –
without their embellishments –
notes are just rain
on the feet of the corpses.

~

Haydn:

Hi there Papa!

Such reticence.

Such politesse.

That's
not the monster
of the personal
on your head?

~

Eric Burdon:

Before *House of the Rising Sun,*
the suffering of Geordies
was material for stand-ups.

~

No point in asking
the mood of the great themes –
whose key is ambivalence.

~

Strings *and* drums:

Where the tiers of the rapt
meet the march-pasts of will,
and hyperbole
t-bones the lot ...

~

In the narrative
of the liner notes,
there is a river
of the deepening of potentials –
which keeps getting wider,
and grander,
the closer it gets to the sea –
till it just disappears –
in a delicate mist –
at the bar of the serial row.

~

Schumann:

Who had more tricks
than anyone:

but whose fingers
all led back to fingers.

~

Mahler (I):

Is this the end of belief?
Or the end of a marriage?

~

Mahler (II):

All the dreams gutted to satire or yearning;
monstered by losses
successors would learn not to see,
he savoured his long journeys homewards:
as if he could daydream salvation – without the belief.

~

The point of modulation
is the site at which
both vistas co-exist:
the site at which
desire confronts reality.

~

Love songs
rise and swell –

as if we sought proofs
in the depths of the mirror –

but dance tunes
lead only to grooves.

~

Shostakovich:

There are desolations
where the narrative remains intact;
and there are those
where story, too, is laid to waste.

~

When silences
ceased being versions of God,
notes became versions of silence.

~

Jazz
never seeks
such control.

But something in classical's
never quite free
of the sadness
of self-conscious minds.

~

Dylan's tunes
can be pure Mantovani –

for the street-cred
of his idioms to refute.

~

For some rockers –
as for the capitalist –
there are only
the twin poles
of loss and desire:

others are rivals;

and *multiples* –
choruses, doo-wop girls –
pillows of aural support;

as for *together*:
how can one offer oneself
as a radiant cock,
in a room tuned to compromise,
justice, good cheer?

~

Floyd, U2:

The urge
to be significant
is like walking the girl
from the floor
to explain
what an excellent
dancer you are.

~

Clubbing:

When the sound system cancels
the difficult gestures of language,
what does it leave
but the judgements of eyes —
the-place-we-can't-live of our genes?

~

Only in Bach:
pattern
that is stronger
than desire.

~

James Brown,
live at the Apollo —
or Mitsuko Uchida,
calming a trill —
both are the music of bodies.

~

Beethoven Quartet Op. 74:

The Harp builds to violence
but veers into beauty: as if to say,
This is the energy beauty requires.

~

When the silence is drowned
by the smother of mannerist style –
it is time to rip things up, and start again.

~

Loneliness, alienation –

but not being sourced in the body,
can electronic music utter grief?

~

Mozart Quintet K516:

As soon as the rhetoric
could signal 'interior' –
tropes for 'withheld' were devised.

~

Elvis asserts love is real,
so the larynx is open.

Dylan asserts
it is past or occluded –
the larynx is closed.

~

La Donna é Mobile:

The Duke is so happy:

You cannot trust women —

you cannot trust women
because they must live
in the system we build and control!

      But: O What a sport!

What a noble eruption
      of motive *and* fun
for those who inhabit
the desolate loggias of power!

~

Elvis reasserted the libido.

But where had it been?

~

So many pieces
regret, in adagios,
what has just been proclaimed
without compromise.

~

Classical (I):

Which started off asking
how far we could travel
and still return home –

but ended
with no faith at all
in the idea of journeys.

~

Classical (II):

Perhaps
its many voices
were anomalous:

we revert
to a music of fragments –
one voice at a time.

~

Some works
are made out of suffering –
and some out of happiness.

Listeners don't care.

As long as it's beautiful now.

~

When there's nothing but music –
　　　it turns into lullaby:

a mother's surround-sound
of car/muzak/ipod

to render us safe
from abrupt, unpredictable things –

to guard us
from *nobody there.*

~

In a culture
　　　intent
on abstracting the self
　　from its moment –
　　　　to recast as statement –

jazz spoke for the moment –

　　　　　till:

liner notes/ articles/ anecdotes. . .
theses/ aesthetics/ CV's –

　　　the great project
　　　gathered its evidence –
storylines, subplots and course-notes –
assessments – farewells.

~

Puccini (I):

As if the tension
in ironic speech,
between utterance and meaning,
had been lyricized
for soprano and strings.

~

Puccini (II):

Whose tenors can't seem to distinguish
betrayals from deaths.

~

As *home*
is defined
by *away*

so home-keys
are pregnant with loss,
and the fear of the moment.

~

The middle-aged prefer
       sedans to hatchbacks –
as Haydn did: balance *and* thrust.

~

Light:

You need courage
to play with a light touch:
Satchmo – the Beatles – Keith J.

Warriors
who understood
that death and generosity are twins.

~

Leonard Cohen:

If what one knows
about feeling
is more potent
than feeling itself,
what can one do except wait
in Victorian rooms?

~

Radio after the war –
Sunday Light Classics play *No No Nanette!* –
Arrangements for Pipe-and-Drum Band :

a triumphant peace,
and an endless confection to prove it.

~

André Rieu and the Adoration of the Matrons:

An overflow
of swings and aprons,
a backflow
of houris and veils –

and a sound from the strings
as of something that Mumsy
had wanted to do
to her very own sweetie-pie, Bling.

~

West Coast rock:

A wide-eyed self-pity
of mellow guitar chords, hot cocoa:

   one ear
on the cold blur of road noise;
the other, half-cocked
for the invite that just will not come.

~

Ravel thought that dreams might be saved
if their phrasing was flawless:

but even the perfect notes vanish –
through mirrors, down marble parterres.

~

Those who rejected the full pitch of opera
were not fazed at all
by the orgasmic throbbing of rock.

~

The authentic
is rock's reply
to *the transcendent*:

neither of which
can be held
in the palm of one's hand.

~

Country and Western,
they say, for Australian distances:

because distance distils us
to needs and regret –

and gestures of beauty and skill
are too small for this sky.

~

Can Brahms's clarinet
still summon loss
in a franchise for Donut Extreme?

~

Pity the mind
that works late in a genre:
that has the technique
to create more emotion
than anyone knows how to use.

~

The fugue knows
you're not so important.

~

No different
from those in the thirties,
who outlawed the Other,
to play, undisturbed,
with Lehár,
in the garden of love –

we, who send the Other to Nauru,
to dress up and flirt,
in the acid domain, with Paul Kelly. . .

~

Having failed
to achieve the transcendent,
some composers
simply took to galloping.

~

Fauré:

Who tried
to work charm into beauty –

but who would not
let death
in the room.

~

You cannot sing a *formal* blues:
pain unknits the hypotactic voice.

~

Ry Cooder:

The calligrapher
does not care
about the quality of the text
from which ink blooms.

~

Masses aside,
          Mozart's
is the first music
not inconsistent
with the absence of God.

~

Bing Crosby:

Avuncular and inviting:
like an ad
for a life without questions.

~

Who speaks
when the orchestra plays?

~

The concerto:

A form from the wars
between self and society.

But what happened after?

Who won?

~

The Dream of Gerontius:

A statement
of its own high intent:
like the king
whose address and comportment
mean more than his words.

~

Quintets and septets and octets:

How many others
can self interact with –
and still remain self?
~

The unassisted voice
is rarely enough now:

Indigenous waif shooed away
from the streets she was born on.

~

Neither the wholly dissonant
nor the seamlessly harmonious
compel the ear:
we prefer to inhabit
the unfinished business between them.

~

If Mahler had only lived longer:
Herbert von Karajan
might have been able to wave to him
over the wire.

~

Bill Evans:

for whom
there were intervals
only heroin could resolve.

~

Like Boxer in *Animal Farm*:
Joe Cocker –
putting his heart in it,
time and again –

while the big wheels
of over-production
talk sessions and dates.

~

A cutting edge, 1966:

On a scuffed, gravel road
past the bus routes,
a loose knot of boys
weigh the rough clothes of *Them*
against scowls from *the pretty things*.

~

Sometimes the romantics
aren't romantic at all –
but simply articulate.

~

An orchestral score
is a management plan for the silence.

As with anything sign-bound, deliberate –
the hard thing's to tease it back
into the warmth of the flesh.

~

The Vivaldi bassoon concertos:

a baroque Charlie Parker –
         on reeds
                  that remind one
that even the unlovely cry.

~

The First Viennese School:

who'd stare as far down
into chasms
as those who came later –

but who'd so much more home
to return to.

~

Here comes the *tutti*:
ignoring – again –
the sadness
of all special pleading.

~

With words:

   perhaps 400 years
   of the subject
   as a field for alternatives;

and notes:

   perhaps 400 years
   of the splicing
   and blending
   of harmonic lines.

~

The Rite of Spring:

When Stravinsky
switched source
from ideal to desire –
the ending changed
from triumph
to exhaustion.

~

With real pain,
the self's integrity
is under threat.

But Lehár pain
sounds like a subject
not getting its way.

~

The rock voice, too,
is a character test.

~

Haydn:

whose music
shaped spaces
his truths would dissolve in.

~

Ravel:

Dramas of tension
between
the controlled
and excessive:

as, in the age of Freud,
climax succeeded transcendence
as the opposite pole
to the daily and governed.

~

The fragment
folds back into silence,
without having broken its surface
with statements
that need to explain their demise.

~

There is a drop of a semitone
        in Guillaume de Machaut
        in Schubert
        and in Paul Simon
which acknowledges a loss,
but holds its nerve –
        interiorisation
at odds with the alt-right universe,
where pain is deflected –
        in the form of a fist –
onto any appropriate other.

~

Simon and Garfunkel: *America*

From when the Americans
still had the courage
to let their young leave
for unknown destinations.

~

Hard to imagine a god
who knows nothing of harmony.

~

If Jackson Browne's regrets
are as abstract as this –
perhaps his desires
weren't so real in the first place.

~

The Hymn:

Another big breath
for the onslaught of will upon song —
as the choir makes its once-a-week way
up the hill of the good ...

~

Springsteen, Richard Thompson, Billy Bragg:

Whose contours and rhythms
are a function
of the price on invulnerability
in working-class speech.

~

Dissonance can destroy a mood —
but it cannot create one.

~

Lou Reed:

For whom neither anger nor lust
could summon the voice
past the safe zone of cool ...

~

Perfect weight
is the most moving thing.

~

The Verdi Requiem:

Neither prayer
nor elegy
but a performance before God –
one that anticipates applause.

~

The Art of the Fugue:

The abrupt finish
of Contrapunctus XIV
shines a void
between construct and world.

~

The Eurythmics:

Annie
stripped the kindness
from her voice
to hear its power.

Men sing like that:
why shouldn't she?

For the same reason other men don't?

~

Tyro:

Straining to manage the note
with his street-voice intact –
lest his street-cred succumb
to the need for an open delivery,
shameful as tears.

~

I never want to hear
those marches again.
I just want to push on –
uncertain –
not trusting momenta –

as if attentiveness
and good intent
might keep us safe.

~

Classical (III):

Which tried to make things sound
as if they mattered –

but whose surest notes
were grief
and the pleasures of utterance.

III

Sisters: Poetry And Music

There are great sighs of yes, but most statements – whether in music or poetry – are negative: they articulate lacks – of power or love, justice or esteem. The problem for the artist is that, by themselves, such statements are one-dimensional. They initiate arcs which may or may not resolve the frustrations they are driven by, but which too often don't look beyond that, towards the subject's others. Hunger takes precedence over the need to acknowledge or explore. As an alternative to such need-driven narrowness, one might posit voices which are outward-looking, and open to the world beyond the self. Rather than being protagonists in a migratory narrative, one might think of them as participants in a dance.

At their best, both music and poetry explore the tension between those voices which derive from need, and those which seek pleasure in interaction. A recurring theme of Western music has been the way that, whenever the iterations of the subject have started to pall, music has turned to the dance: to lighten things up, to make things more bearable – or because we have a sense, anyway, of the necessity of interplay. If the eighteenth century's celebrations of kings and their victories became pompous, then it was time to revisit the *bourrees* and *scottisches* where one could forget power for a while. Once those elegant suites began to sound thin, however, then it was time to explore something meatier: a journey towards ecstasy, perhaps. And when the claims of the symphony became unsustainable, then Prokofiev and Stravinsky could provide us with ballet scores. This is true not just of classical, but of popular music too, which also seems to exist in a tension between dance and the demands of story: from the word-heavy music of the sixties to disco, Madonna and Michael Jackson – and then back again, as the impulse to 'say something' re-emerged with Jeff Buckley or Radiohead.

Neither impulse is enough in itself: we need to push ourselves towards some other place but we also need to interact. Not unsurprisingly, the effect of this is that they endlessly disrupt each other. Too much focus on imagining arrival, and we are just listening to someone's pain, or their yearning for power, or attention. But the dance tunes can be equally inadequate: if they ignore our needs and angers, they soon start to sound trite or repetitive.

The way both music and poetry move between these asymptotes reflects an underlying similarity between them. Compared to this, the fact that some poetry explores the musicality of language is a minor matter: the two forms happen to participate in an aurality which sometimes overlaps. The most powerful link lies in the parallels between their impulses. Both require negativities to drive them – but if either forgets its others, it will not open into spaces the reader or listener can enter as well. Like music, poetry must do more than just engage with its others: it cannot ignore the narratives it is part of – though no other word-based form places the emphasis that poetry does on also turning outwards, into the moment – on dancing, just for the sake of it; on the pleasure and strangeness of doing so. For all the intellectuality of their modes of expression, they are both emotion-based art-forms, and must negotiate the tension between the need to move on, and the desire to engage with the present.

Stave Dreams

The resources of the orchestra seem so much bigger than the creatures who use them. Surely, such range and power are only appropriate for the emotions of gods? A small, comic pedestrian is to be represented by voices which topple into self-importance, if they are not used with the utmost care. A little bag of earnestness has been invited to speak using instruments that abrade the sky. And will take up the offer, without hesitation.

Brahms understood, before his audience did, that Beethoven had failed to summon the eternal, that the project was dead: that composers must henceforth be poets of provisional spaces.

Some repetition is just redundancy. But many of our interactions with the world take the form of repetitions. We live in them: breathing or walking, speaking or making love. Through repetition, we organize the world, and give it meaning. Our lives are built not out of discrete events so much as patterns that vary their frequencies and co-ordinates. To delete all repeats and parallels, as some music does, is to provide nothing for our own patterns to intersect with. A soundscape of unique instances may be entrancing, but we enter it anew each time we encounter it: we cannot build a relationship with anomalies. And just as selves are largely constructed of repetitions, so also are the themes and motifs by which they are projected: which means, for music, that its forms must be repetitive enough to be memorable, and distinct enough for its transformations to be recognised as such. For all the quite necessary explorations of the aleatory and the unrepeatable, music is also a meditation on our capacity to organise our sensory inputs.

Irrespective of how compelling the sound world is, good art also has a sense of its own provisionality. It is aware of itself as art, and never completely loses sight of the world that it came from. It must manage the transitions between the two in such a way as to honour both. This means that listeners must be treated as equals, as opposed to merely being manipulated. The ending must look simultaneously back towards the work, and out towards the world the listener inhabits. If the piece does not handle this transition, it may be a sign that there was something needy in the world it created. For all the magic of Ravel's scores, for example, they rarely summon versions of the 'real', and one must cross a disjunction to leave them. And there is a great deal of less capable work which generates such discontinuities by being self-indulgent, or by using music as a vehicle for display. Once such pieces are finished, that is it: the impulse has been expressed, but only as a private emergency – as a love affair with the stage, or with the sounds the performer has made – and now, abruptly, disjunctively, the listener is set adrift to re-enter his or her own world. No relationship has been established between the listeners' experiences, and the world of the artwork: the artist's needs have been too important. One may or may not have been 'captured by the music's spell', but it did not create a common space in which the listener's presence was implicitly honoured. Too much music is like this – too much human expression: ignoring our commonalities with urgencies grounded in personal impulses – like conversations that bear away on private tangents, barely mindful of the interlocutor.

It is the poetry I hear first, as I become familiar with an unknown piece. As likely as not, it will appear half-consciously, as if it had a subversive quality, and had stolen in beneath my conscious attention. But what does this mean? What does it mean that to my ears, Dallapiccola is a poet, and Birtwhistle is not? I have long thought of poetic language as the realisation of a tension between an understanding and a resistance: between one's sense of the way one would like things to be, for instance, and the way that they are. How this registers in music, I have no idea: perhaps some phrases contain a similar conflict of impulse. Not all composers display this quality moreover, and it doesn't seem to matter much whether they do or not. I am not sure that I find it in either Handel or Verdi – but it doesn't affect my regard for their work. Perhaps 'the poetic' is just a developed idiosyncrasy of the ear – a taste, perhaps, that has gone underground, and developed a life of its own – with a sly capacity for re-appearing, when one is not expecting it. Perhaps, too, it is a kind of luxury: a piece can be powerful or compelling without it. But the impulse that has been taught to sing still conjures a distinctive note, and one still finds one's ear being drawn to it, even if one doesn't know why.

It is sometimes claimed that the best work is made out of our struggle with the night. One should not, however, simply value an artwork according to the bleakness of the material it engages with. We cannot live permanently on the edge of the abyss, any more than we can pretend it isn't there. If one considers the most gothic work – work which cannot shift its gaze from its own distress – it often has a hermitic quality, as if it were the result not of an interaction with the world, but of the obsessions of the artist: a product, not of confrontations, but of avoidances or surrenders. Rather than fighting its pain, it hugs it close. I find this quality in almost everything which valorises the dark above all else: in the songs of Hank – and Lucinda – Williams; in some Tom Waits and Nick Cave; in John Zorn's hardcore-punk phase, and in late Chet Baker. To live only on the edge of the abyss is to have passed beyond the possibility of choice and generosity, and to be helpless before one's needs – as if, having decided that the dark was suitable ground for an aesthetic, one has offered oneself as its captive.

Artists don't have to court darkness: it will find its place anyway in an œuvre. It is, moreover, one thing to write out of difficult circumstances when they arise, but another to stay there after they have passed: Messiaen wrote past *The Quartet at the End of the World*, and Schoenberg did not remain in the mind-set in which he wrote *Pierrot Lunaire*. We have to face in both directions:

we have to confront the dark, but we also have to live with our others, and gesture towards our companions. If light music annoys because it has insufficient gravitas, it is equally true that 'dark' music needs to engage with its others, and to escape from its obsessions. One characteristic of the greatest work is that it moves with relative ease between light and dark. If a piece gets stuck on either note, then perhaps the artist didn't have enough range, enough looseness of heart: hearts can be monotonal too.

The anomie of the later Liszt is in some ways a parallel to the defeat felt by the refugee from modern love. Liszt had wanted to transcend compromise with a passion so powerful, it would absolve him from the egotism that drove it, and the contemporary lover wants something similar. Neither the lover nor the artist *can* transcend their impulses, however: nor will they be absolved of their egotism by giving it full rein. In both cases, failure is accompanied by the conclusion that one must therefore be among the lost. But since nothing was going to save one in that manner anyway, one is not really lost when the expectation collapses. It is the wrong dream now, and it always has been. The plague of modern depression is partly owing to the disappointment of such delusions – the victim still misreading what had happened, but shorn, now, of the excitations the delusions had aroused. If only the suffering were as unreal as the terms of the narrative.

In the Brahms *Hungarian Dances,* there is a disjunct between the erotic lightness of the gypsy tunes, and the richly-harmonised, borderline-pompous 'artistic' pieces with which they are interspersed. If our attempt to construct plausible spaces has struggled, one reason is that we have never found a way past this disjunction. Which mode are you in now? The sexual? Or that more general mode continuous with meaning, status and one's public credibility?

Puccini, said the northerners, wields the dynamic settings too readily; he should wait for the climaxes to build. Mozart, said the Italians, is too restrained: where is his passion? As if the latter thought the reticence of the northerners betrayed a lack of vigour: how could one trust those who did not speak when they thought? But both, really, are emotional cultures: the differences are more a matter of the means and timing of release. Even in their subdued passages, there were few northern composers who weren't aware of climactic possibilities – and they all knew how to delay emotion for maximum effect. In some modes, moreover, the northerners were capable of surrendering to feeling as completely as their southern counterparts. Is there anyone, north or south, who worked at as high a pitch as Richard Strauss? The Schoenberg of *Verklärte Nacht* perhaps – or the Bartók of the first quartet?

As the music became denser, and ever more inventive, freed from repeats and predictable harmonies, one found one could only listen to it consciously: then, it was as beautiful as the work that had preceded it. But it had lost the ability to communicate when its audience was not really listening. The more exploratory and inventive the composers became, the more they were baffled by the limitations of the half-conscious ear. Like poetry, which had also built an aesthetic around exploring the unknown, the work was only available at levels of attention the audience was rarely willing to give it.

Charles Ives, Samuel Barber: sometimes they sound as if they don't understand why they can't speak more freely – as if the relativisation of perspectives in the democratic space restrained the forthrightness with which claims might be asserted. As if, conscious of alternatives – and the respect they deserved – they hesitated to speak with full momentum.

Astonishing that tropes of volition and narrative should have emerged in music at exactly the same time that the capitalist journey became available to the broader population.

Inside the emotion, there is no silence. But the silence emerges quickly enough if the emotion isn't there.

Ravel:

It is the composer's job to shape the score, not the emotion it inflects. If the focus is affect, it will compromise the composer's broader explorations, which is the problem I can have with Ravel: he wishes to manage my response, where most composers are content to allow my responses to emerge as they will.

All artists have a fair idea of the impact of their work. For the most part, however, they are content to let the score speak rather than feeling that they have to micro-manage its effect on the audience. In Ravel, however, there is some anxiety which makes him reluctant to allow this. Neither our art, nor our daily interactions, should be exercises in manipulation. We accept that we should not attempt to control the emotional life of our partners and friends. Equally, the artist should not treat the artwork as a means of managing the audience: it diminishes the relationship from one of a conversation with fellow humans to one of control. One thinks of all those capable people who produce affect to order: writers of TV scores, Muzak-compilers, devisers of sound-tracks for advertisements. Few enjoy a full engagement with either the material or their audience. Not many composers had Ravel's capabilities, and for all his watchfulness, he still left an important oeuvre. But it is hard not to hear the control in his work, and to baulk at its implications for the listener. The care with which he generates the sense of motionlessness – of stagnant repetitition – in *Le Gibet*, or constructs his climax in Boléro, is as much about pre-emptng the listener's response as about generating moods of either horror or abandon, respectively. Rarely does one feel as if one is responding in a way that Ravel hadn't already worked out beforehand. One reason he kept returning to evocations of childhood and fantasy is because of the power they permit the composer: they are themes that do not take emotional risks – as are all stories in which devices such as magic allow the artist an absolute control. Most composers produce their scores in the same spirit as that in which one allows the people one encounters to live their own lives. With Ravel, however, there is something of the manner of the parent. Ultimately, there is a shadow of joylessness over his work, of the refusal of spontaneity or openness, for all the wonder he elicits. And joylessness has always been the punishment for those who seek too much control.

In sonata form, the slow movement became the emotional centre of the work from the beginning – an interiority protected on either side by more public gestures. Later, the romantics emphasised this interiority, and were criticised for it. But the issues it aroused had appeared as soon as the subject had been given a place, and a means of expression. Even the classical composers had had to consider who the self was, in a world which was suddenly difficult to define – the self, as speaker, having become the lens through which any definition might appear.

Wagner, Strauss, Schoenberg: one of the possibilities enabled by great harmonic skill was the representation of hysteria.

In sonata form, the first movement is free to explore as it wishes. But the finale cannot ignore the imminence of its demise.

No self-pity in a fugue, where no voice has precedence over another.

Music is emotion, and – like a crowd – has no memory. In the St John Passion, the chorus which had sung, '*Crucify Him!*' with such vehemence, yields, in oblivious relief, to the peace His crucifixion has bought.

The level of emotionality we accept in a work varies from age to age. It is a judgement we make about both individual pieces, and whole genres or periods, and it is almost the first thing we listen for – a practised and broad-brush review we are scarcely aware of making. Although, at some level, such assessments have an aesthetic component, they are not dissimilar to decisions about the right clothes for an occasion, or the right humour for a particular crowd. One cannot challenge such settings without large confrontations, and the same is true of tastes in emotional register. For a century or more, Mozart was too light. Then the romantics and their successors were too heavy. Change in such matters can be generational, and if one's tastes are out of kilter, one will simply have to accept that one's preferences are, for the time being, eccentricities.

At times, in the twentieth century, when composers needed 'an active principle' for their scores, the only thing they could think of was a march past for epaulettes and clowns.

The Bruckner masses turn the romantic narratives on their head. Tropes which conventionally read for lack are, in Bruckner's hands, the shapes of an imperturbable belief. As unchallenged belief, there is nowhere for their narratives to arrive: there is no lack to be resolved – everything has already been decided. Because, however, they are romantic scores, we keep looking for a question and an answer – while Bruckner just keeps adding modulations. He sounds as puzzled as we are.

In *Tosca* – as in Shirley Bassey, and Celine Dion – the urge to display feeling is stronger than the lack driving it. We recognise this – we have some instinct for unearned emotion – but audiences don't seem to mind: it is the emotion they want; its authenticity doesn't matter.

In one respect, high emotion for Verdi was unavoidable: he was writing for a society in which there were few means by which public differences could be equably resolved. By the time that an argument had emerged, the stakes were already too high.

Harmony is a democratic skill: it creates journeys for equals; it gives voices to others, and invites them to speak. Without it, only one voice can speak at a time.

The most emphatic closures – death, orgasm, triumph – are found in narratives that project the self's anxieties, and since both Classical and Romantic styles were built around subject-narratives, they are the closures they typically resolved to. If, however, a piece is constructed around some other aspect of the world, then such lacks do not come into play: control over its emotional shape – and thus also its ending – is handed to an exterior agency. Neither the seascapes of Debussy, the city-scapes of Vaughan-Williams, Adams or Mingus, nor the 'history-scapes' of Hartmann or Shostakovich arrive at subject-based resolutions. If composers do not believe, any more, that the self can be plausibly situated at the centre of a score, then the audience can no longer expect the 'satisfying' resolutions that the self's lacks require. Scores 'come to a close', or manage neat or lively (or cantankerous) endings – but they can no longer call on their sense of preceding events to provide a 'logical' close. At the heart of this is a transformation in the importance of the subject which is, perhaps, as big a change as any that art has undergone. There is an increasing understanding that one can no longer make one self more important than another simply because the most straightforward way of managing the story is through the audience's identifications. This transformation is incomplete (and may never be completed: most audiences, in most forms, still demand that the self is front and centre). Nevertheless, for those who have understood its implications, subject-based strategies are increasingly seen as artefacts of the way anxiety operates in a text. Understandings and emphases change, but many layers of understanding would have to collapse before artists revert to the traditional perspective on this. One impact of this is that there is now a permanent crisis over the nature of the relationship between the score and the world. Once, the relationship wasn't in dispute. The composer simply needed to resolve the lacks and desires of the subject, which had the advantage – for both artist and audience – of providing a 'natural' set of closures. But now the subject's importance is not central, and we are uncertain of its relationship to its contexts. If we don't know what our relation to the other should be, we won't know how to end the score. At present, I cannot imagine how we will ever know again.

No music got the grief and waste of the last century as well as classical did.

Music entertains every conceivable relationship with the idea of home. Home may be God, in which case, the composer will include a representation of God's presence. It may be an aural and emotional point of rest, one that the rest of the score can play against, as in Haydn. It may be an idealised state – one that, ultimately, one can only gesture towards, as with Beethoven. It may be an elsewhere, or a past state, as with Respighi. It may have been irretrievably smashed apart, as with some of the music written after the second war, or it may be conceptually unachievable, as with Cage. It may be aesthetic: an inspired passage – or, for a jazz musician, a magnificent groove. In love songs, it will be the arms of the lover. For parade music, it may be the thrill of acknowledgement, in the presence of hierarchy. And for some lead singers, it will be the transmutation of one's presence into sexual authority.

The classical impulse – whether in Haydn, Dave Brubeck or Ry Cooder – accepts the negotiation with limit. But the romantic note – whether in Liszt, Coltrane or CSNY – must gesture beyond it.

Some music is disturbed by the experiences it responds to: Vaughan Williams' third symphony is a sick pastoral: it cannot escape his work as a stretcher-bearer; Nick Cave's murder ballads refuse yet distort their lyrical treatment. By far the commonest perturbation, however, occurs when the musical sources are twisted out of shape by the need for assertion and display: repetitions, appoggiaturas, crescendos – *If only there were a simple path to the elevation of my self-esteem!*

Composers have different relationships with the present moment. Some music is defined primarily by its relationship with either the past or the future. In such cases, the present is conceived either as a lack yearning for a past, or for a future of ideals and triumphs: as in Rachmaninoff, or Bruckner, respectively. Other composers rarely lose a sense of the moment they speak from: Mozart, Mendelssohn, Debussy. The latter have sometimes attracted criticism for being 'soft', as if it were an aesthetic reproach that their sense of loss or desire was not absolute. But music is not less because consciousness of the moment has not been overwhelmed by grief or yearning.

Differences in their relationship with the moment are also found among practitioners: some pianists – like Martha Argerich – seem to prefer music fuelled by a meditation on an elsewhere (Schumann, Beethoven); others – Murray Perahia or Mitsuko Uchida – to be drawn to work which, whatever its other impulses, maintains its sense of the present.

The open voice acknowledges its pain, and is prepared to act on it. The closed voice only acknowledges its pain.

Now all the music is available. We have everything except the urgencies of the circumstances it was written in, and the darkness of the future it prayed to.

When Mozart's father or Beethoven's peers complained about the difficulty of their 'learned' works, they weren't just complaining about its technical challenges: they were baffled by the emotions the pieces invoked. The history of difficult art has typically been thought of as a technical matter: sooner or later, the audiences will cotton on, and everything will be happily available within an expanded field of view. But the Mozart 'Haydn' quartets – and all the Beethoven ones – are still a minority taste, even though we have long been exposed to work which is more complex again. Quite apart from the strangeness of the new sounds, audiences baulked at being asked to move beyond the enlargements and doubts of the self's narrative arcs. Why was the trio in K421 so ghostly and interior? Why did Beethoven find it so important to dramatise the impossibility of the ending? As with present-day politics, anything which gestured beyond the anxieties of the subject was dismissed. In 1810, the music was 'too learned'; now, ideas may be 'elitist', or 'affected': any term will do, as long as one doesn't have to engage with the threatening and pointless territory beyond one's self-importance.

Eliot said that poetry was language which approached the condition of music. But it could equally be said that music – a great deal of it at least – is sound which approaches the condition of language.

Bach's themes unfold in the presence of God: they are underwritten by His love. But when Bach's successors set out on their individual narratives, they introduced doubt into the score: that they might not arrive where they hoped; that it was the right kind of journey in the first place. The work of each new generation could be defined by the way in which it attempted to answer the questions thrown up by its predecessors. Eventually, however, there were so many narratives, conjuring so many questions, it became impossible to manage. How could one define oneself against so many possibilities? For much of its history, inventiveness in classical music was prompted by doubt – but the doubt won.

Where are the choruses of despair? Does the close interaction required of massed voices preclude it?

If you say yes, you must have someone to say yes to. The lack of an interlocutor makes it difficult, now, to write music of praise.

Tchaikovsky can announce an emotion as if it were a point of arrival. But it can't be. Emotions are inherently unstable: their purpose is to seek a more stable position – to express themselves out of existence.

We often overlook how hard the composers pleaded for the rectification of lacks we no longer share. The critical focus has been on transcendence, but in many scores the greatest emphasis was simply on a fairer earthly existence – from *The Magic Flute,* to *Fidelio* and *The Masked Ball.* Even the Beethoven Ninth is partly just a prayer for *better* – for an earthly revolution. Now that many of the political rights that the composers could only dream of are in place – universal suffrage, for instance, or freedom from arbitrary arrest – we sometimes struggle to respond to their vehemence. Such things are part of everyday life now. What was all the fuss about?

The first decision of the audience involves how much emotion it is prepared to engage with. Mostly, the answer is: not very much – its members have to live, they can't afford to let their timetables be disrupted. So most music is either light in tone, or, if the emotional pitch is high, projected in such a way as to indicate that it is a stage emotion, and not meant to be unsettling. Easy to say that this is a weakness: that everyone should engage with challenging things – though kinder, perhaps, to say that our not doing so is just a characteristic frailty, a by-product of the things we must do to survive. Even if one despairs about the morality of attention, and its underlying programmes, there is little one can do about it: one cannot ask people to re-invent their self-justification. But it makes those with a willingness to engage with more pretty valuable: always small in number, they become the archipelago of the receptive the musicians write for.

The problem of how one should end a piece is the same as the issue of what one can say. The ending, after all, is just its final assertion – its summarising gesture, or moment of negotiation with the silence.

Variations grew out of improvisatory traditions – opportunities for display and virtuosity. As such, they contain a self-conscious element which removes them a little from the momentum of the piece as a whole. One takes time out to enter a more aestheticised space before the journey resumes. Rather than participating in an agon, one is asked to take time for inventiveness and its effects. One has stepped off the train to enjoy a presentation.

Contemporary music rarely invokes triumph or failure: its edges are not so well-defined. One might say rather that it oscillates between energy and anomie. Triumph requires a narrative to fulfil: we may daydream, but rarely now believe in the claims that would allow such satisfactions.

Twentieth century Spanish music is often characterised as picturesque and atmospheric. But there's an unhappy necessity underlying its soundworld of elsewheres: all those *back-thens*, and *over-theres* are the gestures of a culture in which one was seldom allowed to confront the present without restrictions.

Johann Heinichen wrote entrance-music for August the Strong of Dresden. It has been praised for its vivacity, but no-one now remembers the lively effusions of the Prince-Elector's other servants, nor the pleasing shapeliness of their flourishes, and it is hard to see why Heinichen should be regarded as special, just because his flattery was achieved with distinctive aural skills.

They had hoped that their skills and inspirations would take them on a journey to a brave new world. When they found out, however, that they had not left the place they had started from, the only thing they could think of to do was to dance.

Electric Dreams

In the progress of taste from Wagner to Madonna – as transcendent endings gave way to abandoned ones – the centrality of the subject remained unchanged. Transcendence, after all, had partly been an attempt to keep our narratives intact – to create a place where the self could still be viable. And the abandonment rock seeks still imagines that after one has trashed oneself, one will still be there tomorrow – albeit in a state requiring renovation. Pop throws up an endless stream of subjects who fill the world with their anxieties – who cannot, that is, imagine their non-existence – even when their sublimations ultimately lead to the disintegration of consciousness. Neither transcendence nor abandon imagines beyond the centrality of the self by inviting the other to dance in a way that really acknowledges the other's existence.

Post-war, nothing marked the advance of democracy more than the way the working classes were given permission to suffer. One of the main expressions of this was in rock: first, the acknowledgement of desire (*Dr Feelgood, Midnight Rambler*), and then the certainty of loss (*Angie, Broken English*). Prior to that, the workers' requests had been rightly refused: it would only make them unhappy. Their lives were hard enough already, without any encouragements to dwell. There was, rather, an arrangement of musical compartments constructed to manage an awkward situation. For those who must struggle to survive: light romance, musical comedy; a few (turn-a-blind-eye-to-these) drinking songs; and then – something to honour the tribe with – decorous gestures of triumph: mildness as an expression of imperium. And for those who could afford it: an occasional indulgence in the theatre of disturbance – a little Aida, perhaps – or, if that was too much: the chuckle and confirmation of G&S.

There is an æsthetic in rock which resists warmth of feeling lest the edges around need and loss aren't defined sharply enough. Tolerance and generosity – or so it is felt – interfere with the capacity to drive the song strongly enough. The last thing the rock musician wants is an ill-defined interplay between willpower and kindness: not when the song's most important need is to define a hunger.

One reason given for trying to kick the doors down in the sixties was in the hope that feeling might be allowed: it was done, so people claimed, out of a desire to be real. But feelings have to compromise, at some point. We have to imagine the other, too, and interact with it. We cannot just keep sounding the note of the self: the world and its inhabitants must also be allowed to speak. At some stage, we have to create a music in which desire and awareness of the other are both present – in which assertion and acknowledgement are not contradictions.

Over and over, from Bruckner to the Alan Parsons Project, we have been invited to believe that emphasis was revelatory – a kind of proof, surging from one apotheosis to the next, as if the answer were an orderly sequence of fortissimos.

The rebelliousness in which rock was steeped gave it energy, but it was not necessarily a promising basis for musicality. If musicality requires a dialogue between voices, in order to avoid being one-dimensional, that is not well-served by asserting one voice at the expense of others. Some rock did become little more than tantrums in rhythm – theorised by the tantrum-empathy of its commentators, and reinforced by the decibel-authority of the speakers. The problem for rock was to take a relatively simple form, a form always ready to fall back into mere assertion, and to find a way of creating a place for the other within it. But they did it – instinctively and without theory: from the liquid invitations of the guitarists, to the studio inventiveness of a Tony Visconti or a Dave Stewart; from the play of multiple voices in The Beachboys or The Band, to the complexity of the great rock voices, whose roughnesses and inaccuracies created ways for the voice to sing against itself – and thus admit alternatives, and imply its others – out of the layering of tone which already existed in colloquial speech.

If one of the most fertile veins which opened for rock was as a meditation on the possibilities of the colloquial voice, then it is unlikely that we will see another 'rock revolution' – the colloquial having been relieved of the burdens which gave it credibility, and deployed by the corporate world as the facetiousness which forgives all abuses.

When I was a kid, I thought rock was about risk and possibility. Now, I wonder at how low the mood of so much of the best stuff was: Neil Young, Joni, Dylan – and then: Nirvana, Jeff Buckley, Elliot Smith. As if, like the confessional poets, its sexual ambition could only ever have led to overwhelming losses – that for all its energy, its dreams were of a conquering sexuality, and impossibly corrupt. It is not unique in this, and has been more honest about such things than the society whose equally corrupt dreams it sings. But it opened the door on an impossible set of dilemmas, and whatever the answer, it won't be more glamour: more lasers, more bass.

If you excoriate New York life as Lou Reed did, you will not be able to turn your judgement into song. At least part of the song must slide inside the life it sings about. But this level of condemnation is incapable of such sleights: it will not relax beyond the Sprechstimme of malediction.

People don't go for the song, in rock, so much as for the whole package of the definitive version: the sound-textures, the vocal inflections, the jizz of the group. Occasionally, someone will attempt a variation on a well-known tune, but mostly, working with the material of others means presenting a repeat of the famous version. Perhaps the moves of the champion singer appeal to them – and the adulation that goes with them. The word 'cover' is used, as if the song were an old mare, awaiting the same approaches that had worked so well before. But cover groups are admired only for the faithfulness of their mimicry: that is the most they can aspire to. As ever, there is little that is democratic about art: no opportunity here for the punter to join the ranks of the elect just by playing charades with enough verisimilitude.

In a film score, the lead instrument is the action.

When music and language occur together, the music rules the space in which the words are perceived. Mostly, it will leave only enough room for brief and loosely-connected phrases, though sometimes – as in folk-songs – it will step back enough to allow syntactic coherence. It will never, however, leave so much room that there is space for language to be tensioned against itself, as in a poem: that requires silence. If the lyrics look flat on the page, that is because they are waiting to be brought to life by the music – as opposed to the poem, which must have the muscularity to sustain an independent existence.

The song that interrupts itself to talk has little faith in music.

We are too busy to appreciate music which offers alternative voices, or engages with its others. We have just enough wherewithal for music which drives onwards, as we are driven, towards goals, necessities and dreams of enlargement. We want regular rhythms and voices that are decently paced but not headlong. We don't want phrases where the will wavers, which invoke a sensuality we cannot pause for, or which imply that the destination is not important. In our urban spaces, our most characteristic use for music is as soundtrack: we play narrative-momentum music, on the nominal theme of love.

The human note is not enough to sustain the song. It must tap into the fierceness the human tries to manage; it must find a momentum which is stronger than regret.

Classic versions of any music are just about impossible to replicate. But the variables which must intersect to make a rock song great make the form particularly dependent on the circumstances in which it is created: the right musicians, instruments and voices; the right producer, studio and technicians – to say nothing of the right mix of emotional inflections, and musical ideas. Once the track has been set down, moreover, its conjunction of gestures will never again mean what it did at that moment. No doubt one could put together a good cover of 'Hey Joe'. Except that Joe is going to 'head way down south, where a man can be free,' – and now the border has changed: it is crawling with uniforms and presidents. So has the nature of police enforcement: the fugitive must first evade the data bank, and the internet. 'Ain't no judge gonna put a rope around me,' he says, but in the twenty-first century, hanging is a cruel and unusual punishment. No guitarist now, moreover, has one foot in the chitlin' circuit, and one in what was then the strange new world of pop. And no contemporary voice is likely to contain the reticence one hears in Hendrix, as if he were unsure whether he really had permission to be on stage in what was still a white person's world. 'Hey Joe' only had one moment to be itself in. And, if anything, this has only got worse: the rate of change has meant that the act of recording captures ever more evanescent and unrepeatable intersections of technology, culture and musical impulse.

Was there ever a genre that developed and matured as quickly as rock?

Rock was a way for the middle-classes to participate in the rawness they had left behind, in pursuit of choice and insulation.

The advent of amplification meant that the increase in volume that had once signalled a heightened degree of lack was no longer inherently associated with physical effort. The link between volume and level of emotion remained as a trope: Shirley Bassey still reached for the big notes; many songs – from 'You've Lost That Lovin' Feeling' to 'Stairway to Heaven', were still built around the connection. But there was an increasing sense that this was a contrivance – that volume was a function of the mixing desk. Increasingly, also, the dial was being set at the one level for the whole song: it became more important for the music to carry in a narrow range, one level above the road noise, than for it to explore the changes in expression one could exploit through shifts in dynamics. Needing a means by which to express variations in intensity, musicians explored tightening the voice rather than opening it: the narrower the larynx, the greater the emotion. Other things were at play as well – this overlapped with the attempt to express feeling within street conventions – but for perhaps the first time in the West, we developed a semiotics of the constricted throat.

'Pop' is no longer an adequate term to describe the range of genres it has spawned, many of which now function in scenes as obscure, and with audiences as small, as anything that classical works with.

Rock is a music of sexual urgency – and it needed to be: too much popular music had been merely polite. But it is a limitation of rock that it so rarely turns its gaze beyond such things – the obsession with loss and desire can also be a moral myopia.

Some of the more emotionally generous music in rock (The Beatles, The Band, Crowded House) – music which looks beyond subject and object to the third party as well – also displays an inventive use of language. Its capacity to convey generosity is largely a function of its lyrics, but it is hard not to think that the multi-stranded nature of its harmonies doesn't owe something to the multiple centres of gravity in its words.

There was a period – between, say, 1965 and 1975 – when tastes in popular music in the US and the UK overlapped. But then they went their separate ways. Why? The British reacted viscerally against the optimism of the period, as if it was sappy, or delusional – or as if they were angry that they'd allowed themselves to be conned. But the States – apart from those pockets of punk in the cities – largely seemed to have gone on their way unruffled. Their period of darkness and reaction came later. Perhaps the optimism of the period did not feel out of place against the American Dream, whereas in Britain, it came up hard against a class system that had barely shifted. And now the two cultures seem further apart than ever. They can converse at the level of their idealisms, but the circumstances of survival for the ordinary person are increasingly different, and their respective imaginations reflect this. The way, for instance, in which the two cultures would use the word, 'reasonable', would only partly overlap.

Popular music operates with many of the tensions and impulses that drive classical. It too begins in the assertion of an idea which is very like a statement, and contrives ways of playing against it with counter-voices and antitheses – though it tends to do so by adjusting its voices, rather than through musical structures. It also maintains a dialogue between music which originates in language, and music which inflects towards dance. In sonic terms it is probably even more experimental than classical: anything that can be incorporated will be. But it remains restricted in what it can do in terms of form. There are no pop equivalents to the journeys of either sonata form, or those romantic or experimental narratives, in which a musical impulse transforms itself through a range of emotions. It is rare for a pop song to explore more than one emotion, or to consider an emotion from more than one perspective. When it does so, it often feels contrived, as with *Bohemian Rhapsody*, or *MacArthur Park*. It will explore sequences – thematically unified albums – in which individual songs each operate as a single facet of a complex idea, as in a song-cycle. But it seldom builds musical ideas through time – laying them against each other, and finding ways to make them interact. Some of this has to do with the way the different genres are conceived: working with a score has obvious advantages when it comes to managing complexity. Some of it has to do with the form: most songs are brief. But there are also imaginative reasons: we have become reluctant to conceive of our lives as a single coherent narrative. We trust the fragment – the expression of a moment – but are increasingly less willing to believe in structures that combine them.

Music has de-coupled from the spaces it is produced in. Once, microphones recorded actual performers in spaces with distinct characteristics, and the result was partly an expression of the space. There were different acoustics in different rooms: from jazz-clubs, where echoes were absorbed by the bodies, to cathedrals, where they were built into the score. The music was also produced in distinctive social spaces: one can hear the working-class aggression in the early Beatles, and, later, their buoyant, innocent expectation that the barriers would come down soon. From Haydn at the Esterhazy's, to Django Reinhardt in wartime Paris; from 'The Last Post' at Changi to 'The Quartet for the End of Time' in Stalag VIII, it has been almost impossible to separate the music from the space it was created in. But now it is being de-contextualised. It is composed in offices in Tokyo and classrooms in New York by people who are based – but only briefly – in Chicago and Madrid. Its aural contexts are also disappearing. Electronic depths of field are different to those produced instrumentally: to the listener, they may still project onto different parts of the sound-stage, but they carry no sense of physical origin. Electronic work can sound like the realisation of an interiority. This, no doubt, is little different to all the other ways in which place no longer exists, and it will probably not be noticed for very much longer. But one of the pleasures of music, in an age which allowed it to move beyond its physical origin, lay in one's sense of the links between the music itself, and the context it came embedded in. No doubt there will be other pleasures, and such connections may come to be seen as no more than a quaint but minor artefact of the First Age of Recording. Rather than being an extra dimension of the aural moment, they will become the abstruse details that cultural historians spend too much time on. Someone toward the back, her Total Music Electrode turned down low, may smile at the innocent physicality of the primitives.

Both classical and rock are genres which are founded in statements – or their musical equivalents. We cannot lose our capacity to make them: they are how we assert ourselves against chaos. But by themselves, they are rarely enough: repeated, they soon become monotonous. Like kids who can't help themselves, we must disarm or enliven them with dance, humour and lyricism – and so music becomes a dialogue between the vigour and one-dimensionality of assertion, and the slant and evasive pleasures which make it bearable.

So much contemporary music – from minimalism to dance – is *pulsed*: as if we are at the end of an arc which evolved from meditations on eternity to understandings that are wholly temporal.

Too often now, music is just the industrial manufacture of status, using an aural (and visual) semiotics, rather than one built around financial or physical prowess. At its most talentless, it can be less honest: some of the wealthy, after all, have had to put their own money together – and people in sport do have to be good at their game.

As genres mature, the question of how best to perform a well-known body of work arises. Some artists are able to see past the sophistications of the present to the impulses that originally drove the music. This is not something for tyros. Only people who have spent a long time working within a genre seem able to do this: Ry Cooder's old fifties rock numbers; Gianluigi Troversi's popular Italian melodies; Clapton's explorations of Robert Johnson – and the decades-long meditation, in jazz, on the American songbook. It is not available in the early days of a style: there's too much uncritical enthusiasm, and too many possibilities still to explore; besides, there isn't enough distance yet, between artist and song, for the work to be visible.

Music of desire and loss, like rock, speaks to singular, personal needs, its audiences being collections of individuals – of interiorities – rather than communities. Other genres – classical, for instance, or folk – project into communal spaces. One implication of this is that whereas folk and classical often have a positive relationship with their pasts – consistent with the way communities, ideally at least, treat both dead and living with respect – rock, particularly in its early years, had little historical sense, each new crop of heroes being set against anyone who challenged their status. This is not to say that communities of fellow-feeling didn't emerge in rock. But one of rock's functions was to provide musicalised sexual displays, and thus, as with all courtship, its musicians came to regard each other as rivals. Other styles and performances became unworthy of notice. Fashions – in music, idiom and dress – took on a heightened importance: demarcation lines separating those with credibility from those with none. In this respect, rock could sound like an endlessly shifting pronouncement on tone. In those genres with a greater sense of their own communities, however, where the music was addressed not to a multitude of needs, but to an audience of peers, it was less acceptable to reject people for reasons of taste. Perhaps there was less hormonal edge to prompt the gestures of exclusion. And speaking to our socially-constructed selves, which can be more forgiving, it was often easier for the music to find things in common with other voices.

Bjork, PJ Harvey: not songs, but dance-tunes with voice accompaniment. The protagonist is the bass, so there is little option for the voice other than to be acquiescent – and hence child-like. And since disempowerment creates grief, it is fitting that the mood is low.

All that light music, on either side of the war – from Lehár and Jeannette McDonald to Doris Day and *The Sound of Music:* a klieg-lit vapour of displacement accompanied by the smother of frills on the pelmets and the ever-so-careful arrangement of excellent legs. But no sex. Sex didn't exist even after the commitment to pay the mortgage had been confirmed with a ring. Astonishing how this ballet for chipper disguises could keep its shape in so many contexts, needing only to be sung to by the occasional light baritone, or straightened up and freshened, by the first four bars of the strings.

In the 1960's, by telling stories beyond the anxieties of the self and its desires, folk offered a music of the third person. Prior to that, acknowledgement of pain in pop had only ever been an acknowledgement of the self's pain – no other pain existed. With the stories of others, however, awareness could turn into compassion, and a concern for justice. By extending pop's moral universe beyond the subject, 'Eleanor Rigby' and 'A Day in the Life' became possible – together with the worlds of Dylan and Springsteen. Musically, folk may not have brought much to the table that was not already present, but by creating a space for more complex lyrics – where the other could be heard as well – it invited pop into the adult world. It did not take long, moreover, for this new complexity in the lyrics to require a more complex musical expression.

Rock is a music of the voice. With the exception of some guitar solos, instrumental passages must be short – otherwise the fans switch off. Mostly, the purpose of the instruments is to frame the voice as compellingly as possible. Rock songs are verbal gestures – language embedded in and enhanced by drumbeats and guitar contours.

For all the good music out there, the bulk of it is inattentive, repetitive and one-dimensional. Somehow, the system still works: the sound-waves keep getting extruded; no-one listens too closely – and no-one seems affronted by the absence of anything more. The artists get their money – and the general impression is that the background noise displays admirable buoyancy – albeit in a somewhat needy tone.

Syncopation, in jazz, isn't just a different way of doing rhythm. It signals an alternative conception of music to the statement-based forms such as classical and rock, where some phrases are taken so seriously they can only be enlarged and repeated; where lines are drawn in the sand with one's vehemence; where some themes cannot be relinquished until their limits have been reached. Syncopation says that *these* notes are going to initiate a passage of play; that any assertions may not be taken seriously by the offbeat; that the body – particularly the hips – will also be invited to this party. That any attempt to ground utterance in the questionable certainties of words may be undermined by a moment of ironic delay. There is a connection, moreover, between the pauses of syncopation, and the independent-mindedness of improvisation: they both suggest that interpretation will be on the musician's terms.

Just as early photos of Montmartre show a dusty slum with bedraggled trees – hardly the place where a revolution in art was occurring – so images of the UK of the sixties do not invoke the blues-inflected, LSD-coloured experiments that were being produced there: the rainy streets with pillar-boxes; the boys with their ties and jackets; the workers streaming out of the yard at knock-off time. The American images could be more plausible – this was, after all, where the music originated – but it is still a jump from, say, Newport in 1964, or kids with their crew-cuts at a drive-in, to 'Desolation Row' or 'All Along the Watchtower'.

Punks were a product of urban environments – of the world of artefacts which comes in only one of two conditions: intact or broken. And so they could rage with confidence, knowing that any imperfections in their surroundings were absolutes that justified large aggressions. Nothing, on the other hand, could be more inappropriate than a punk in a natural setting, where such black-or-white distinctions are absurd. In nature, there are only the subtle gradations of growth and decay. No imperfections there, no failed ideals. No point in searching for the right-sized safety-pin, if you're out with the songbirds and beetles.

Great jazz or classical voices are distinctive. But the great rock voices are distinctive to the point of idiosyncrasy. They are mostly self-taught, so there is little homogenisation from having learnt in a developed tradition – though they must have listened to each other's work, and figured out, at the very least, a vocabulary of the things that work. Despite that, it sometimes sounds as if their styles developed in contexts that were completely isolated from each other. No doubt each set of instruments, each cultural moment, each set of rhythms *was* distinctive. But that was true of the jazz and classical singers too. One difference may have been that the rock singers had to negotiate between the musical demands of the song, and the need to be colloquially plausible – to shape voices that had street-cred. Perhaps, given the different accents, classes and regions they started from, this extra consideration produced the extreme variation one hears between Elvis and Dylan, Patti Smith and Amy Winehouse, Bowie and Elvis Costello.

Northern Soul was the expression of a technological moment: the pressings were just cheap enough to be produced in small numbers, but difficult enough to replicate for the rarity factor to apply. Any earlier, and too much would have been involved in the production of the discs. Any later, and they could simply have been copied.

It is difficult for music produced without input from the body to be invested with the weight of human lack. Increasingly, if we wish to register pain or vulnerability, we must find a way to disrupt the seamless output of electrical energy with our imperfections. But how can one interact with the perfect and invulnerable? Sounds generated by the body can only play as afterthoughts against it. We can dance to this impervious output, but if we try to sing with it, the vulnerability in our voices makes us sound diminished in comparison. One solution seems to be to make the voices stylized:

either crazy, or mechanical, or with a forlorn awareness of the impossibility of matching such power – though in such cases, we are adapting to it, not the other way round. Without being able to articulate our vulnerability, moreover, there is no way to structure a release from it: no way of imagining *home*. Without tropes of home to guide our navigation, the music sounds locationless: it doesn't come from anywhere and it doesn't need to arrive anywhere else – which may be appropriate for a planet that is hurtling around the Milky Way at 200kps, but is not helpful if we are trying to create some temporary shelter – which is one of the functions of art. There are disempowerments in this new world of flawless momenta. Dismay at their imperturbability has quietly become one of our characteristic griefs.

How can one represent agency without embodied expression? Without musicians making choices about the way to play their instruments? When the only input the music needs is that of a hand sequencing a keyboard? The body has been abstracted from the process, and the music – having been produced without physical cost, or with the cost hidden deep beneath the transformations the sound undergoes – is unable to tap into the emotion only bodies can express. Many possibilities have opened up. But not the representation of agency. Agency is meaningless without decisions about costs – it *is* the expression of such choices. Without the weight of the body, however, there are no costs in the creation of music: there is simply ratiocination. Why should an audience care, if there are no costs for it to identify with?

One has to go back to the cabaret artists of Berlin in the thirties before one finds popular musicians who are as dismissive of their culture as Lou Reed or Randy Newman are of theirs. These are not just occasional expressions of artistic mood. Such angers are only possible when there are real despairs to provoke them.

Some audiences don't need a causal link between situation and emotion. They are happy just to jump into a bath of generic arousal. There can be a fear in this, however, of the demands of the narrative: better to dwell in an effusion of the lush and over-emphasised, where such things don't matter – the adults can deal with things later.

Some musicians – Chopin, Duke Ellington, the Beatles – speak from an ambiguous location which is neither public nor private. Everyone has had to work with such ambiguities, from time to time, so we understand its two-way inflection, but it is not a place we typically feel settled in. It is, however, a strangely potent place to speak from. It is as if there were a poignancy in groundlessness – a shiftlessness we respond to, that some part of us trusts. Perhaps we attend more keenly, half-listening for the point of rest we know isn't there.

It is not a bad thing that Australians are hopeless at singing the anthem. Better that than that they sing it lustily, with their eyeballs rolled back, and their brains tuned to *follow*.

To begin with, the hair, drugs and bad grammar had been almost as important as the sexual drumbeats, and the improbably eloquent guitars. Now, fifty years later, rebellion is just a convention, and artists who had once been rivals, sit in the same room, and admire the same riffs. Rock no longer faces outwards, towards society, but back, towards its history. Now, you need access to a body of knowledge just to locate what you are listening to. Rock CD's are accompanied by musicological commentaries that match those given to jazz or classical music. As for the contexts it emerged from – they, too, are becoming historical: to be retrieved by research, or glimpsed in oral histories. The music will not be forgotten – there will always be the curious and the connoisseurs – but to the casual listener, it will sound like faintly familiar birdsong.

Word/Body

There are pervasive differences between jazz and rock. Many rock fans resist jazz rhythms deeply. Nor do they like improvisation. Conversely, even when rock is much more than the mindless loud strumming it is characterised as in the less flattering descriptions of jazz fans, the jazz buffs will still find it difficult to hear past the predictability of its bass lines and drums.

The two forms have different roots: with jazz – the syncopations, the blue note, the improvisation – and the reeds and horns; with rock – the guitar aesthetics, the highly pitched emotion and the passion for amplification and display. But the biggest difference is that language is woven into the texture of rock in a way that isn't true of jazz. One might say that words are present at the conception of the rock song – whereas jazz typically has a more intimate connection to the impulses of the body. A corollary of this is that rock readily takes the form of an assertion, whereas jazz – ultimately, perhaps, because of the impatience of the body with the strictures of meaning – is at the very least mistrustful of such things, and usually happy to undermine or play with any assertion it finds in its sights.

The earliest rock'n'roll was largely sourced in the body too – but that willingness to let the body take the lead didn't last in the hands of white musicians and their audiences, as rock'n'roll segued into rock. The early white American rockers, together with their British cousins, were so steeped in a culture of statements – of measuring themselves against their capacity to make language come true – that the combative, four-square rhythms which assertion required soon replaced the lighter, more flexible rhythms that Elvis and Bill Haley had inherited.

It was also significant that rock was appropriated by the young. Their first duty – particularly as young white males of the sixties conceived it – was to assert themselves. One can do this with music alone, by drawing attention to one's distinctiveness, and by dissing the techniques of one's predecessors. But such distinctions do not travel easily beyond the cognoscenti and the practitioners. If you want to make sure that your claims are not misinterpreted, it helps to express it in words. Rock singers became specialists in the making of claims – on either their own behalf, or for those for whom they sang: 'Hope I die before I get old,' or, 'You don't believe we're on the eve of destruction,' or just: 'Sex and drugs and rock'n'roll.' Like few genres before it, the power of the rock-song came from the tension between its assertions, and the social space it was sung into. Verbal assertion, moreover, is inherently inflexible – which exacerbated this tension – unlike, say, a musical phrase, which is always open to a change of direction.

Rock songs, moreover, are built around the qualities of a voice. The subtleties in rock came not from the play of its assertions in a field of arguments and counter-assertions, but from the semiotics of the voice it lay them down with. Thus, for instance, the rock voices ironized quickly – layering an innocent gesture with overkill, say, to create the undercut in Lennon's 'And so this is Christmas' or Elvis Costello's 'She's filing her nails/ while they're dragging the lake.' Our capacity to listen for such things stems from our everyday expertise with the weight and credibility of the utterance. The great singers learnt when to play it straight, and when to qualify their own assertions, and the audiences grasped these nuances quickly, because they'd already had so much practice with ordinary speech.

Compared to practitioners in jazz or classical, many rock musicians – at least in the first generation – did not have a background in music. There were a few who thought with their instruments – Hendrix, Jimmy Page perhaps, Keith Moon – but many of the songs seem to have been conceived as contours improvised between speech-rhythms, and the smallish number of chords the musicians could play. They took the few scraps of controllable sound that they knew, and worked them up into a tune. Language was an essential component of the conception of rock songs, in a way that had rarely been true of either the earlier popular music, or of jazz. The lyrics of the American songbook and Tin Pan Alley, for instance, were mostly written in response to tunes that had already been composed

A few of the writers of rock lyrics, somewhat astonishingly, quickly became more ambitious than the writers of popular music had ever been before. The lyrics of Ira Gershwin and Noel Coward had been witty, and nuanced, but they had never explored the range of metaphor or perspective that some of the rock lyrics did. There is nothing in the songbook like 'Nowhere Man,' or 'Desolation Row.'

Sometimes, the rock voice took the whole spotlight, and sometimes it allowed the guitar a solo. Jazz, on the other hand, rarely foregrounded the lyric. In the earliest jazz tunes, the singer only got a turn about three verses in – and was lucky to be given more than one verse. The lyrics could be subversive – there was plenty of double-entendre – but they were seldom confrontational in the way rock was. No doubt it was difficult for African Americans to be too direct until the sixties, when changes in society started to make it possible. When they were, jazz could certainly be assertive – as with, say, Ornette Coleman or Nina Simone. But it seldom seemed willing to sustain the note of aggression in the way rock would – almost as if its accompanying sense of alternative possibilities were a natural release valve. As for the lyrics themselves: mostly, they seemed to be viewed as a potential source of play – though there were exceptions such as Simone's 'Backlash'. Audiences, moreover, have always been ambivalent about singing in jazz. Many jazz fans do not like jazz singing: words get in the way of appreciating the instruments; they inhibit their freedom of play. Lyrics come in a set order, and with set rhythms, but one has come, they say, to hear freedom of expression. Jazz singing is a genre of its own, an essential element of the world of jazz – but it is a little to the side – a mirror equivalent to rock instrumentals, which are also not quite part of the main game. As for the sort of focus on words one finds, say, in Dylan, that is unthinkable: the long stanzas are an impossible restriction on inventiveness.

Jazz, moreover, has often favoured instruments which parallel the range of the voice, but which have strengths and flexibilities of their own: which are, in other words, a kind of open challenge to the presence of the singer. In the array of voices one finds in a jazz combo, the singer is only one among many.

Although one can be angry in jazz, there is an instinct for pleasure in the body that gets tired of insisting – that seeks a homeostatic restoration of balance once the anger has been expressed. But language and willpower go together. Assertion wants to sustain the note, to be inarguable, to outlast. It has lack, rather than pleasure, to drive it – and lack is stubborn. There is a sense in which, if the audience doesn't assent to the assertion in a rock song, the song fails – if the song doesn't have enough expressive momentum, for instance, or if it feels too 'light'. The aesthetics of rock place great store by whether lack has been realised with sufficient 'heaviness' – a heaviness commensurate with the scale of lack in the listener (it does not value small lacks: they are regarded as trivial). Jazz, on the other hand, invites the listener to share in the pleasure of its interactions. Anything which takes pleasure in itself has an inbuilt leaning towards forgiveness. To the extent that jazz originates in the body, it carves positive presences: contours without insistence or implication. At some level, however, an assertion is built around a negative: it wants the listener to grant the claim or surrender to its power. The rock fan cannot understand the pleasure with which the jazz musician explores the possibilities of the song. It is not important enough, this delight: it defines no position, it articulates no hungers. But to the jazz musician, it is the reason for getting one's instruments out.

Acknowledgements

With thanks to the editors of *Meanjin* ('The Finales'), *Australian Love Poems* ed. Tredinnick ('Mick: *Satisfaction*'), *Heat* ('Mahler in Midsummer'), and *Island* ('Caravan Park'). 'Word/Body' appeared in the newsletter of the Jazz Action Society (May 2011) and, in a form closer to that printed here, in *Sotto*, the e-magazine of Australian Poetry Ltd. A number of these poems have appeared in the following collections: earlier versions of 'The Singer' (as 'Portrait') and 'Schubert Sonata' in *In the Cage of Loves Gradings* (Island, 1997), and of 'Symphony' and 'Riley Lee' in *Sensual Horizons* (Five Islands, 2001). Two minims ('Janis' and 'It can utter ridiculous things . . .') also appeared first in *Sensual Horizon*. 'The Goldberg Variations' and 'Hawkesbury River' were first published in *The Human Project* (P&W, 2009). 'The Bach Chorale' and 'The Country where Nobody Sings' were first published in *Ground* (P&W, 2015).